Written &
Art Direction By
CAELA COLLINS

Illustrated
By
JEN YOON

MILL CITY PRESS

Mill City Press, Inc.
2301 Lucien Way #415
Maitland, FL 32751
407.339.4217
www.millcitypress.net

Printed in the United States of America.
ISBN-13: 978-1-54566-175-8

Illustration by Jeongin Yoon
Cover art designed by Caela Collins
Art Direction by Caela Collins

Visit http://www.caela.org/

Please contact Author via email:
CaelaBooks@gmail.com

To those who are
brave enough to find
an adventure around
every corner and seek
the unseen...

This is Catori, she's 6 years
old and she isn't afraid of
anything. Not big dogs, not
thunder & lightning, not
heights, not the dark; not
even falling down because
she knew that getting
scrapes and bruises only
made her stronger. Catori
is fearless, brave, and has
a huge imagination.

She is a true adventurer.
Sometimes she's a pirate at
sea, going on scavenger
hunts in the rain for
treasure. Some days she's
an archaeologist in the
sandbox, finding new
things like ancient pottery
and digging up old
dinosaur bones. In some
ways she's a spy, ducking
and dodging motion sensors
in the toy store's pink aisle
in order to get to the
action toys.

Every summer Catori stays with
her grandma, where she has the
best adventures. Sometimes Catori
would travel through the jungle,
collecting wild berries and snakes
from her grandma's garden.

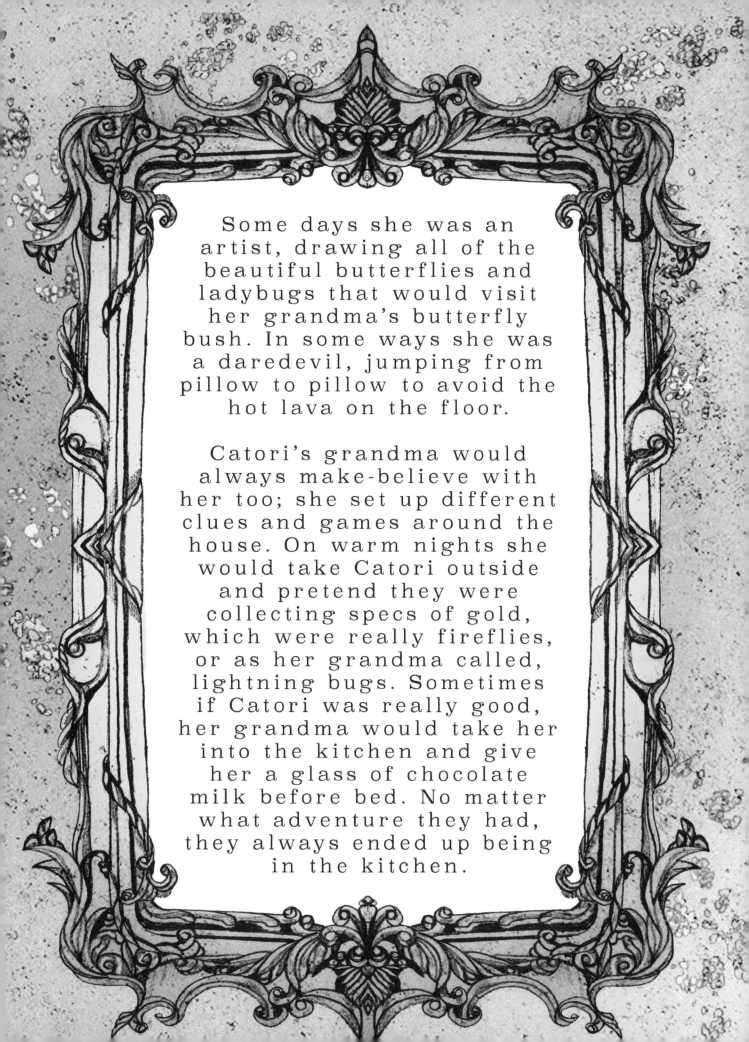

Some days she was an artist, drawing all of the beautiful butterflies and ladybugs that would visit her grandma's butterfly bush. In some ways she was a daredevil, jumping from pillow to pillow to avoid the hot lava on the floor.

Catori's grandma would always make-believe with her too; she set up different clues and games around the house. On warm nights she would take Catori outside and pretend they were collecting specs of gold, which were really fireflies, or as her grandma called, lightning bugs. Sometimes if Catori was really good, her grandma would take her into the kitchen and give her a glass of chocolate milk before bed. No matter what adventure they had, they always ended up being in the kitchen.

Catori loved her grandma and the time that they spent together, especially in the kitchen. Whenever they finished their adventures they would always cook together.

Catori loved helping around the kitchen because that meant that her and her grandma could use their scrap-cookbook, which Catori called the Scrookbook! Together they would make new recipes, draw pictures of the food or designs for the cakes that they baked, paste lots of stickers, or play hangman and tic-tac-toe while they waited for the food to cook. Most importantly, they wrote down all of the fun adventures they had in the Scrookbook. It was the best part of the day—Catori and her Grandma were like wizards in a castle, mixing potions, and together they would laugh. Catori loved her grandma.

Before bedtime her grandma would give her a big-big hug every night, and Catori would put the Scrookbook under her pillow for safekeeping, in hopes that some of the make-believe adventures would come true.

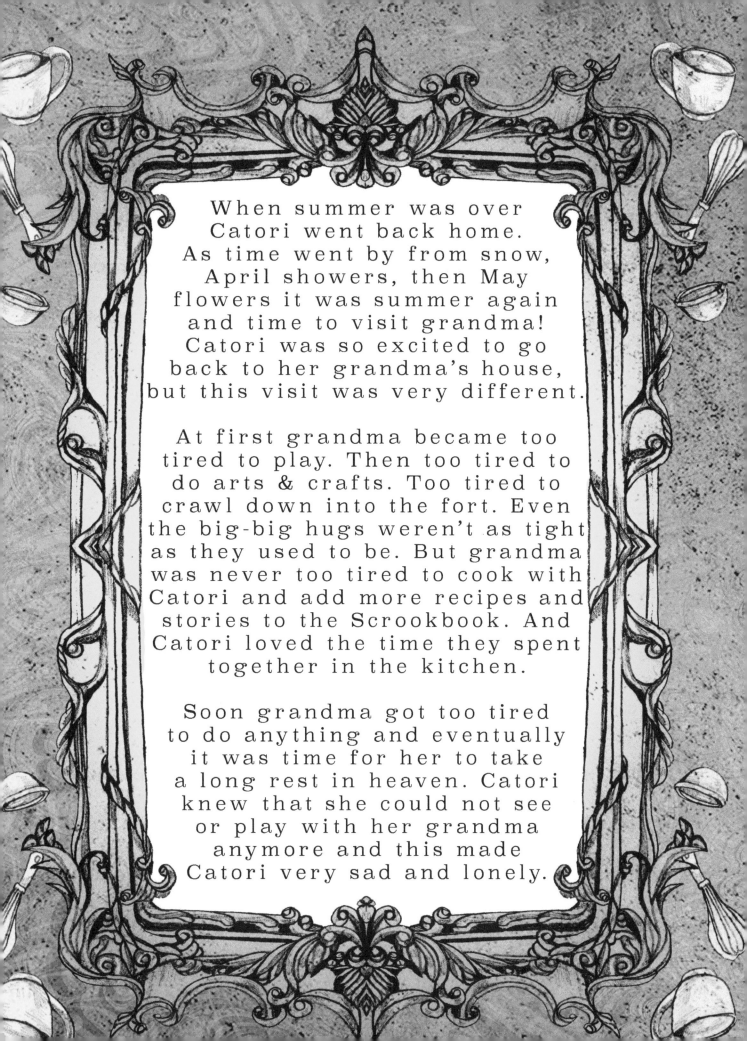

When summer was over
Catori went back home.
As time went by from snow,
April showers, then May
flowers it was summer again
and time to visit grandma!
Catori was so excited to go
back to her grandma's house,
but this visit was very different.

At first grandma became too
tired to play. Then too tired to
do arts & crafts. Too tired to
crawl down into the fort. Even
the big-big hugs weren't as tight
as they used to be. But grandma
was never too tired to cook with
Catori and add more recipes and
stories to the Scrookbook. And
Catori loved the time they spent
together in the kitchen.

Soon grandma got too tired
to do anything and eventually
it was time for her to take
a long rest in heaven. Catori
knew that she could not see
or play with her grandma
anymore and this made
Catori very sad and lonely.

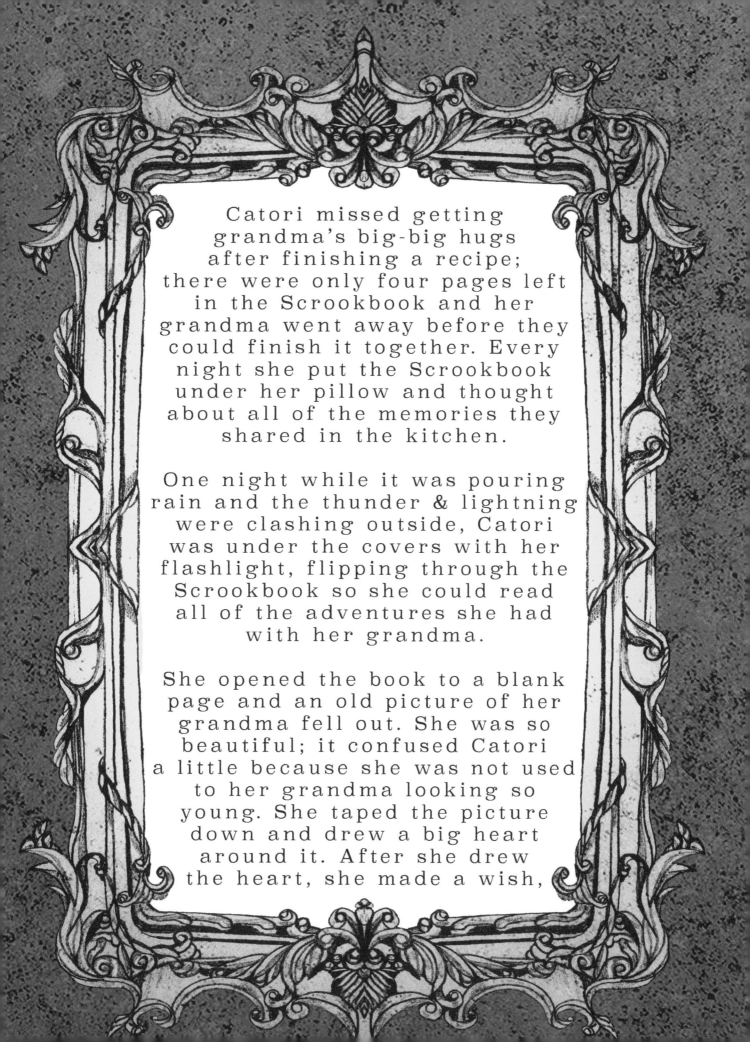

Catori missed getting grandma's big-big hugs after finishing a recipe; there were only four pages left in the Scrookbook and her grandma went away before they could finish it together. Every night she put the Scrookbook under her pillow and thought about all of the memories they shared in the kitchen.

One night while it was pouring rain and the thunder & lightning were clashing outside, Catori was under the covers with her flashlight, flipping through the Scrookbook so she could read all of the adventures she had with her grandma.

She opened the book to a blank page and an old picture of her grandma fell out. She was so beautiful; it confused Catori a little because she was not used to her grandma looking so young. She taped the picture down and drew a big heart around it. After she drew the heart, she made a wish,

Recipe

2 cups flour
3/4 teaspoon salt
8 tablespoons butter
10 tablespoons ice water

8 cups sliced apples
2 tablespoons lemon juice
3/4 cup sugar
1 teaspoon cinnamon
2 tablespoons cornstarch

"I wish I could have
one more adventure
with my grandma
so we can finish the
Scrookbook together."

Before Catori changed
into her pajamas
she fell asleep and
forgot to slide the
book under her pillow.

She was so sleepy that she
even forgot to close the book
or turn off her flashlight.
BOoM! CrACK! Were the sounds
that the thunder & lightning
made as the flashlight started
to flicker and the heart she
drew around her grandma's
photo began to glow.

Start

By: Cato

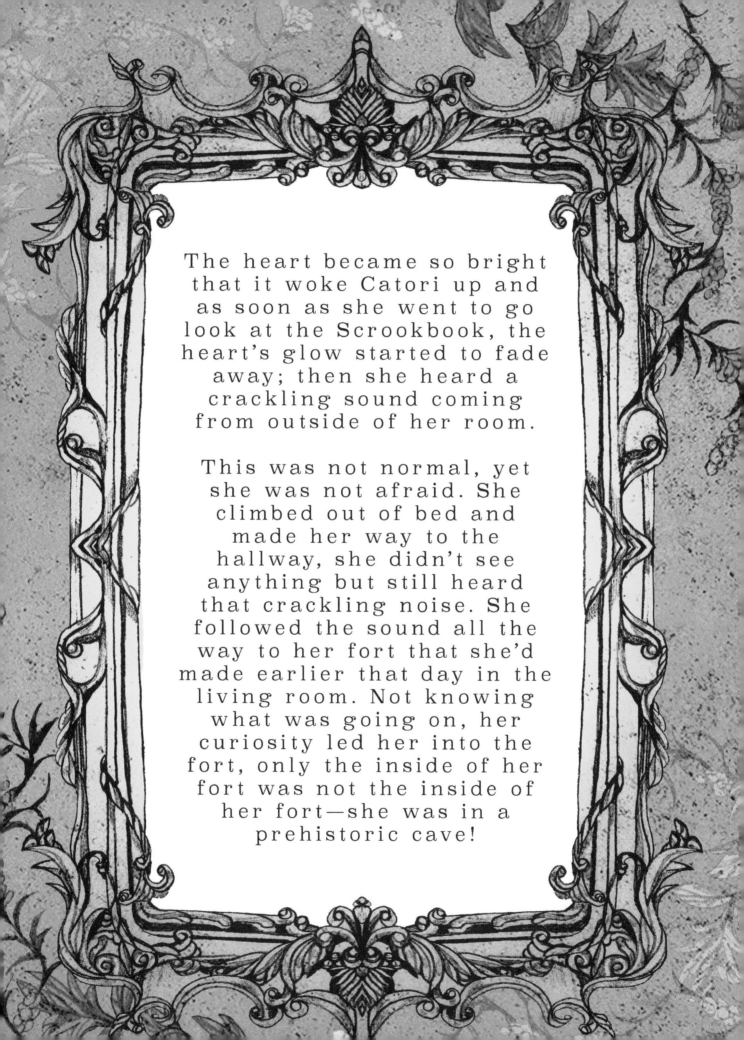

The heart became so bright that it woke Catori up and as soon as she went to go look at the Scrookbook, the heart's glow started to fade away; then she heard a crackling sound coming from outside of her room.

This was not normal, yet she was not afraid. She climbed out of bed and made her way to the hallway, she didn't see anything but still heard that crackling noise. She followed the sound all the way to her fort that she'd made earlier that day in the living room. Not knowing what was going on, her curiosity led her into the fort, only the inside of her fort was not the inside of her fort—she was in a prehistoric cave!

She ran her fingers across the rocky walls; she couldn't believe that she was inside of her fort! At first, she thought it was a dream and pinched herself only to find out that she was not dreaming at all—This was real.

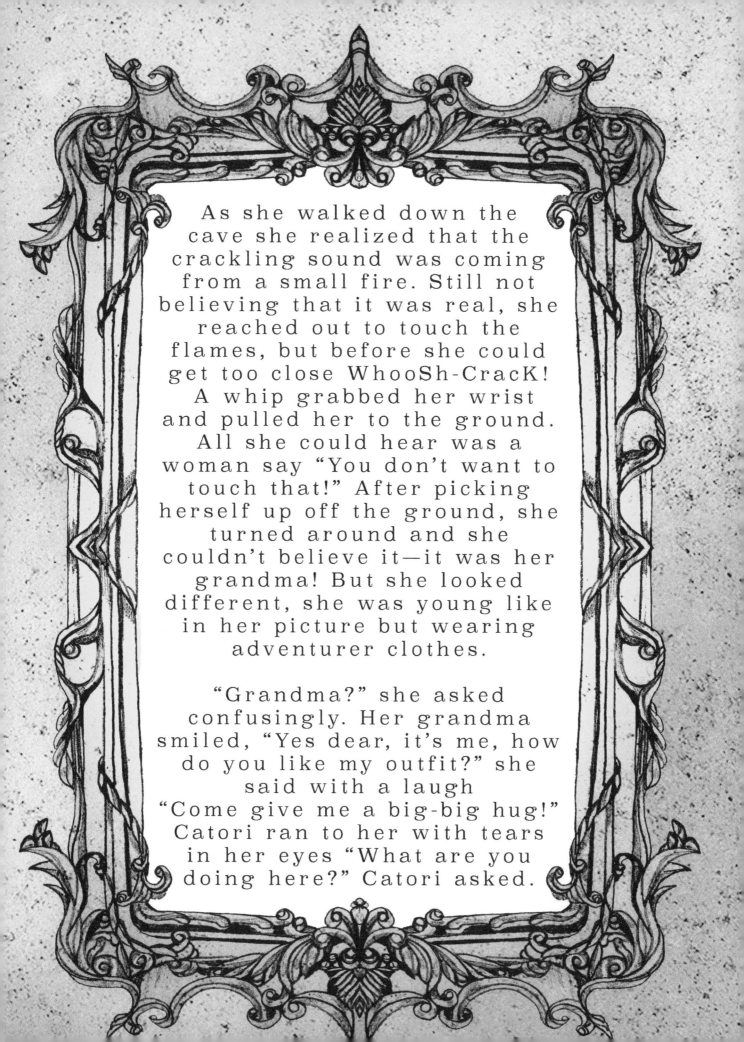

As she walked down the cave she realized that the crackling sound was coming from a small fire. Still not believing that it was real, she reached out to touch the flames, but before she could get too close WhooSh-CracK! A whip grabbed her wrist and pulled her to the ground. All she could hear was a woman say "You don't want to touch that!" After picking herself up off the ground, she turned around and she couldn't believe it—it was her grandma! But she looked different, she was young like in her picture but wearing adventurer clothes.

"Grandma?" she asked confusingly. Her grandma smiled, "Yes dear, it's me, how do you like my outfit?" she said with a laugh "Come give me a big-big hug!" Catori ran to her with tears in her eyes "What are you doing here?" Catori asked.

"I'm here to grant your wish"
her grandmother explained. Then
Catori remembered the wish that she
made before falling asleep—to spend
one last adventure with her grandma
and finish the Scrookbook. The
glowing heart, the old picture,
the thunderstorm, and flashlight,
it all made sense!

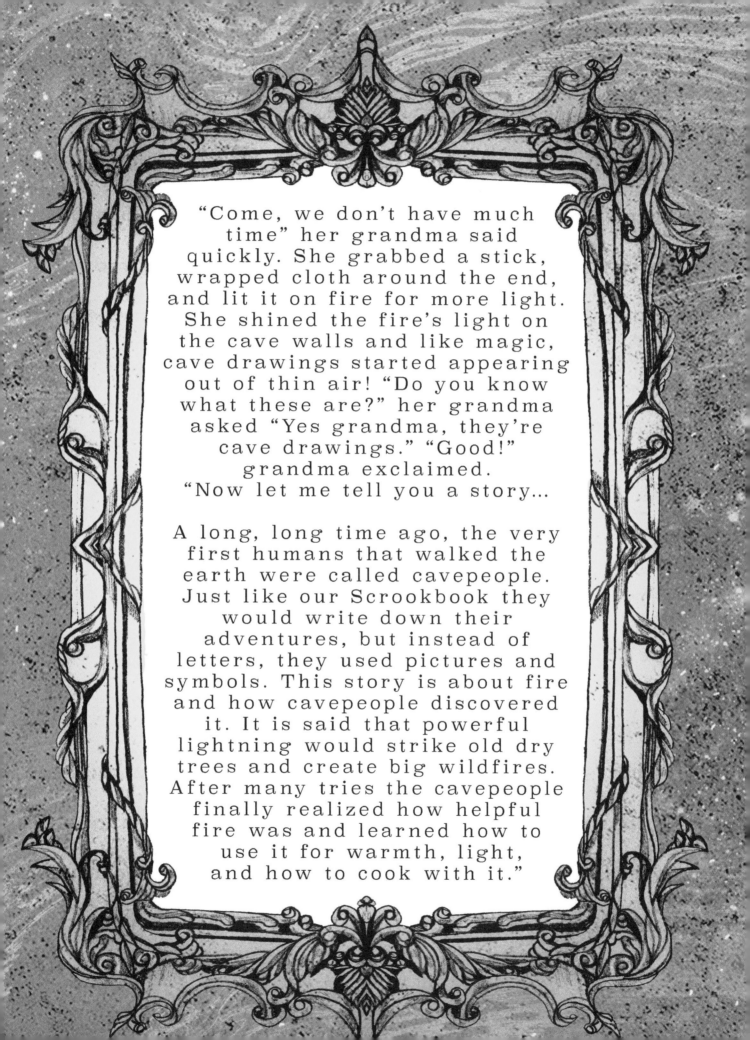

"Come, we don't have much time" her grandma said quickly. She grabbed a stick, wrapped cloth around the end, and lit it on fire for more light. She shined the fire's light on the cave walls and like magic, cave drawings started appearing out of thin air! "Do you know what these are?" her grandma asked "Yes grandma, they're cave drawings." "Good!" grandma exclaimed. "Now let me tell you a story...

A long, long time ago, the very first humans that walked the earth were called cavepeople. Just like our Scrookbook they would write down their adventures, but instead of letters, they used pictures and symbols. This story is about fire and how cavepeople discovered it. It is said that powerful lightning would strike old dry trees and create big wildfires. After many tries the cavepeople finally realized how helpful fire was and learned how to use it for warmth, light, and how to cook with it."

"Fire is a very powerful thing that is both dangerous and beautiful. For the cavepeople fire was a sign that they were going to eat. We are the only living creatures that learned how to cook with fire. When the cavepeople learned to cook, it changed the history of food forever."

"This is the first lesson of tonight Catori and that's why I'm here. In order to finish the Scrookbook you have to understand the history of food. That's why..."

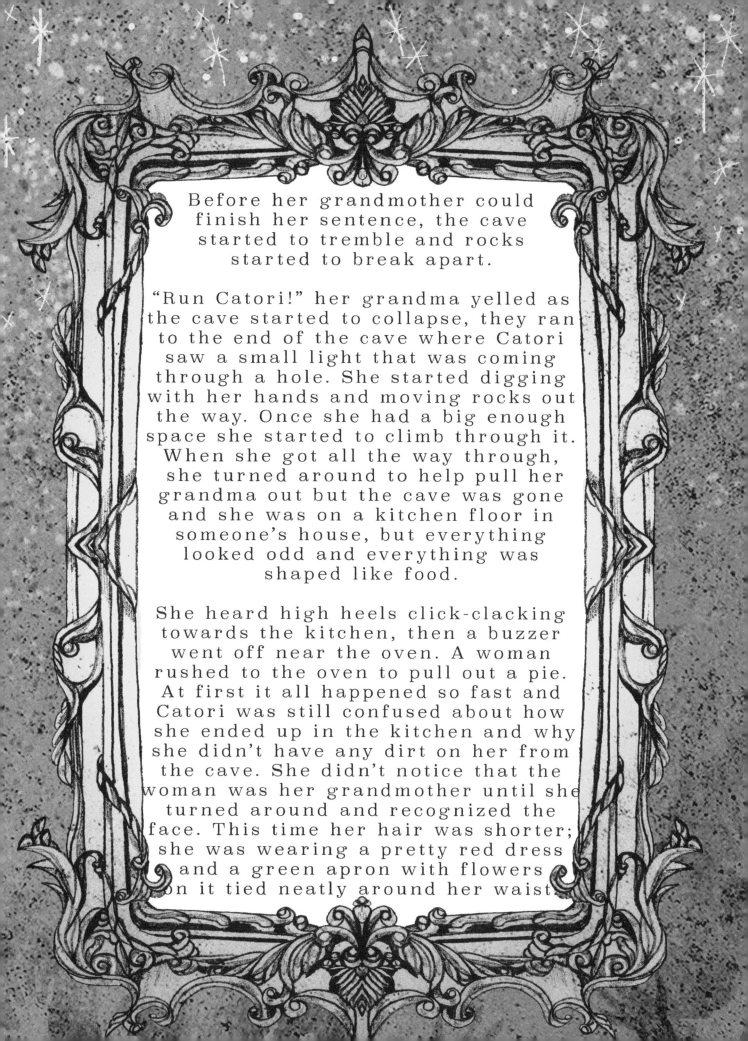

Before her grandmother could finish her sentence, the cave started to tremble and rocks started to break apart.

"Run Catori!" her grandma yelled as the cave started to collapse, they ran to the end of the cave where Catori saw a small light that was coming through a hole. She started digging with her hands and moving rocks out the way. Once she had a big enough space she started to climb through it. When she got all the way through, she turned around to help pull her grandma out but the cave was gone and she was on a kitchen floor in someone's house, but everything looked odd and everything was shaped like food.

She heard high heels click-clacking towards the kitchen, then a buzzer went off near the oven. A woman rushed to the oven to pull out a pie. At first it all happened so fast and Catori was still confused about how she ended up in the kitchen and why she didn't have any dirt on her from the cave. She didn't notice that the woman was her grandmother until she turned around and recognized the face. This time her hair was shorter; she was wearing a pretty red dress and a green apron with flowers on it tied neatly around her waist.

"Hi Sweetie." Her grandma said. "You look different; How did we go from a cave to a kitchen?" Catori asked with a confused look on her face. "This is the second lesson honey, from fire to the oven" her grandma answered with a kind smile.

Catori walked over to the table and sat down while her grandma brought a piece of pie over to her. "You learned the importance of fire, how it was created, and how it helped us survive. As time went by humans started learning how to read, write, and make new inventions that hold heat and create something similar to fire like ovens and stoves. Without fire we wouldn't have ovens. The cave you were in was about 1 billion years old, now we're in the year 1950, where pretty much everything is handmade. This pie was handmade. I used ingredients like flour, eggs, and water to make my own pie crust from scratch and even the apple filling, which I washed, cut, and cooked apples with cinnamon, vanilla bean, ginger, and other spices. Most of the vegetables I make for lunch and dinner are from my own garden out back. I make it all by hand without any frozen or canned foods. Although we've come a long way from a simple fire, in the 1950s we still take the time to make everything ourselves, we call it homemade."

Catori was amazed at how food and fire changed over time. "Can you grab the milk from the refrigerator Catori?" her grandma asked "Yes ma'am." Catori walked over to the refrigerator and reached for the bottle of milk way in the back.

She was finally able to grab the milk, but to her surprise when she closed the refrigerator door and turned around, she wasn't in the kitchen anymore and the milk that she had in her hand turned into a shopping basket. Catori was in a grocery store, but everything looked older than the stores she was used to. Was this another lesson? She thought.

She walked through the frozen section and then the baking aisle; she saw rows and rows of TV dinners, frozen pie crusts, and canned fruit and vegetables. Once she made it to the register she saw her grandma again, this time she was the cashier; she had a bun and was wearing a white and grey dress with a black turtleneck. "Put your stuff on the belt please." Her grandma asked as she winked.

When Catori emptied her basket she noticed that everything was premade from frozen meals to ready-**made** cake mix.

"What do you notice that's different?" her grandma asked

"Everything is already made or cooked." Catori said "Yes! This is the third lesson. It's 1970 and more people are cooking food that is already put together like cake mix and spaghetti sauce. It's easier and quicker than making it all by hand. Earlier in 1967 the microwave was invented, which claimed to be "The greatest discovery since fire." Soon it began to replace ovens. It became a flameless electronic way of cooking which gave people a lot more time to do other things."

Before Catori could say anything, her grandma handed her a brown paper grocery bag with her premade items inside. "See you soon Catori," her grandma waved. Catori walked outside the door and heard a Beep-Beep! "get in!" a woman yelled.

It was her grandma again for the fourth time, this time she was wearing a sparkly head wrap and driving an old purple-ish car that turned different colors in the light like a mood ring.

Catori hopped in and asked
"Where are we going
grandma?"
"Is this the fourth lesson?"
"Yes, honey, there's not much
time so let's get to it!"

Catori jumped in the car and
her grandma drove her to a
drive-in theatre where they
served hot dogs, hamburgers,
and popcorn. "It's 1974 Catori
and during this time a lot of
people watched movies in their
cars during the summer. Fast
food car stops were very
popular because they made food
that was quick, easy, and that
everyone liked. It took place of
being in the kitchen
altogether."

"So, we went from fire, to
ovens, then to microwaves, and
then drive thrus?" Catori asked.

"Yes. These lessons were to
show you how important food is
and how it has changed so
much over time. When we cook
together we are creating
memories from our hearts.

Although a lot has changed, each
version of cooking is special in its own
way—new ways make new traditions.
Cooking food is an act of love and
that's why this is our last adventure.
I want you to know that the **Scrookbook**
is something to remember me by and
know that my food is love."

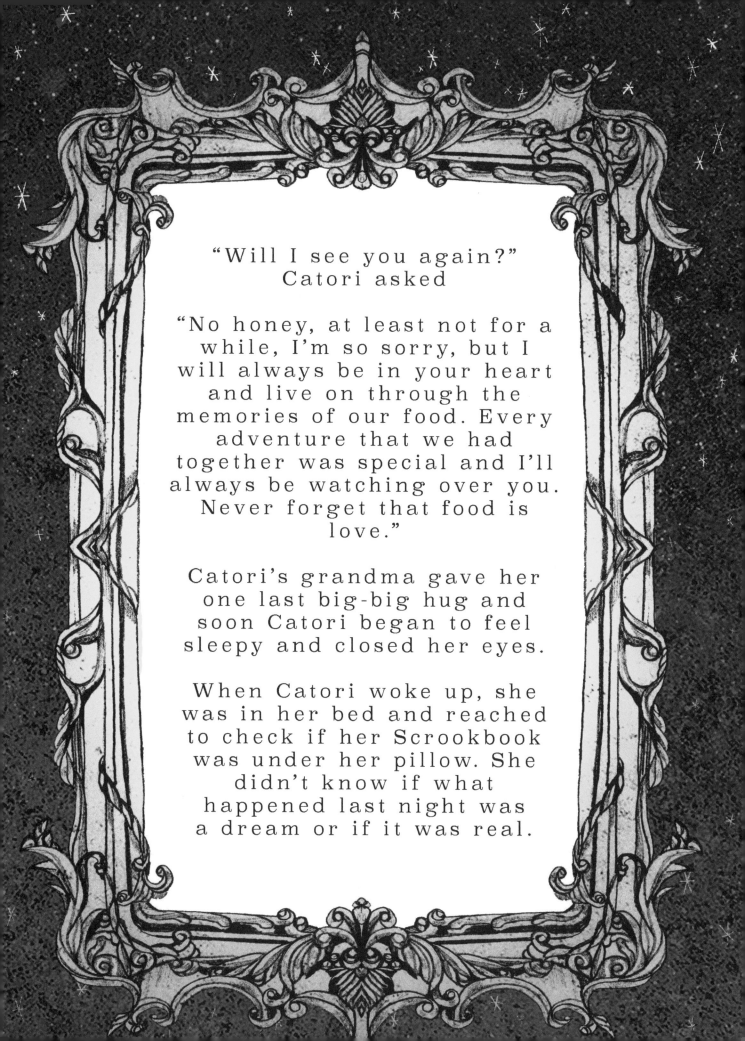

"Will I see you again?"
Catori asked

"No honey, at least not for a while, I'm so sorry, but I will always be in your heart and live on through the memories of our food. Every adventure that we had together was special and I'll always be watching over you. Never forget that food is love."

Catori's grandma gave her one last big-big hug and soon Catori began to feel sleepy and closed her eyes.

When Catori woke up, she was in her bed and reached to check if her Scrookbook was under her pillow. She didn't know if what happened last night was a dream or if it was real.

She began flipping through the pages of her Scrookbook and when she reached the end, the picture of her grandma wasn't there and the Scrookbook wasn't finished. There were still four blank pages left.

She felt disappointed that her wish didn't come true. She closed the Scrookbook and walked over to her window and saw the mailman coming. She went downstairs to grab the mail from the mail slot on her door and noticed a red envelope with her name on it. When she opened it, the same picture of her grandma that was in the Scrookbook fell out. She picked it up and saw that there was an apple pie recipe on the back and that was signed "Food is love- Love, Grandma." She then pulled out a letter from the red envelope and it was a story in her grandma's handwriting of the 4 lessons and the last adventure they had.

Catori couldn't believe
it, it was all true, it
really happened last
night! She ran upstairs
to put the story in her
Scrookbook and saw a
gift wrapped on her bed.
It said, to Catori from
Grandma. She tore open
the wrapping paper and
it was a new Scrookbook
that said Food is Love
in big gold letters
on the cover.

Catori understood the
four lessons that her
grandma taught her
and realized that in
order to keep her
grandma's spirit
alive, she had to show
love through food.
Ever since that day
she never stopped
Scrookbooking.

About the AUTHOR

Caela Collins is a writer, art director, and conceptual & mixed media artist from Connecticut. She is a Business graduate who minored in Public Relations and Studio Art at Marymount Manhattan College.

Her goal is to fuel imagination through wonder & awe and inspire people to be adventurous.

~

Website:
https://www.caela.org/

E-mail:
CaelaBooks@gmail.com

About the ILLUSTRATOR

Jen Yoon is an award-winning illustrator who graduated with an illustration BFA at the School of Visual Arts. She specializes in digital mediums, combining traditional materials.

~

Website:
https://www.behance.net/jeonginyoon

~

E-mail:
Jeongin.Yoon.00@gmail.com

~

Instagram: @Jenyoonart

CPSIA information can be obtained
at www.ICGtesting.com
Printed in the USA
BVHW022259260619
552049BV00006B/7/P

9 781545 661758